D1128766

THE ROYAL IN FOCUS

IN WORLD WAR II

Part Two

Lt Cdr Ben Warlow RN

In this second volume of the Royal Navy in Focus in World War II, I have delved into my own archives to bring a miscellany of the ships that fought that long and arduous war. There are one or two from other collections - credits being given with the texts. The Navy was desperately short of ships at the outbreak of the war, but would have found itself in an impossible position had it not been for the short period of "peace in our time" during which a tremendous construction programme was started. Suddenly shipyards, which had been starved of orders a few years earlier, were working flat out to build battleships, aircraft carriers, cruisers, destroyers, escorts, minesweepers and submarines. This fever was to last for over six long years, and only slowed when the war was brought to a sudden end by the dropping of the Atomic bombs on Hiroshima and Nagasaki. By that time at least a few of the older ships were being laid up to permit the manning of newer ships, an indication that construction had outstripped losses. Nevertheless, the price paid during those six years was high, both in ships and in men. It is hoped that this collection will bring back happy memories for some, and show to to a younger generation to some extent the variety of ships employed and tasks carried out by the Royal Navy during those important years. The majority of these photographs were taken during the war.

Ben Warlow
Burnham-on-Crouch
August 2002

First published in the United Kingdom in 2002 by Maritime Books, Lodge Hill, Liskeard, Cornwall, PL14 4EL

ACHILLES

The light cruiser ACHILLES came to public notice in December 1939, when she, her sister ship AJAX and the cruiser EXETER were in the action which led to the scuttling of the German battleship ADMIRAL GRAF SPEE. During the action she was damaged by shell splinters. Afterwards she returned to New Zealand (as she was with the New Zealand Division of the Royal Navy) and then operated in the Indian Ocean until February 1942. She then joined with Australian and American forces operating off the New Hebrides. In January 1943 she moved to the South-West Solomons. Whilst withdrawing from an operation her X turret was damaged by a bomb. She was repaired in the UK and in March 1944 joined the Eastern Fleet, and afterwards the newly formed British Pacific Fleet. In May 1945 she operated off the Sakishima-Gunto Group of islands and later off Truk, and took part in attacks on the Tokyo and Yokohama area. She returned to the UK from New Zealand in 1946. In 1950 she became the Indian Naval Ship DELHI and finally paid off in 1977.

ALYNBANK

The ALYNBANK was a Bank Line general-purpose cargo ship built in 1925. She was requisitioned in October 1939 and converted to an Auxiliary AA ship, with four twin 4-inch HA/LA, two quadruple 2-pounder, two 20-mm and two multiple machine guns. She initially covered shipping in Home Waters and in May to October 1942 escorted convoys to Russia, her AA armament proving very effective. In October 1942 she moved south for the assault on Oran and later took part in the Sicilian and Salerno landings, being hit three times. She returned to the UK to pay off, but was re-activated for the Normandy landings, where she was used as the first block-ship in the Mulberry B harbour, being sunk off Arromanches on 7 June 1944. She was raised in 1945 for breaking up.

AMPHION (15 February 1945)

A new class of submarine, based on the successful T Class and embracing the lessons of the war. She was built with a view to the long range operations required in the Pacific War and developed in 1944/45. The AMPHION was the first to complete in March 1945, and after trials and work up sailed from the Holy Loch in September 1945 to Bermuda and Trinidad, returning in November 1945. These 1,120 ton boats had a surface speed of 19 knots, and a dived speed of 8 knots with an endurance of 10,500 miles at 11 knots. They were armed with a 4-inch gun and ten torpedo tubes. Two were built with this low bow, but they, and the rest of the class, were fitted later with buoyancy tanks forward, altering their appearance. She was the first A Class submarine to visit the Far East and Australia. Later she was streamlined and eventually broken up in 1971.

ANNAN (25 September 1944)

The ANNAN represents the many ships of her class that fought successfully in the Atlantic and Pacific. Originally called "twin screw corvettes", they were renamed "frigates" at the suggestion of Canada's Chief of Naval Staff. Many were built in Canada. They represented a vast improvement over the Flower Class corvettes, being larger (1370 tons), faster (at 20 knots), better armed (two single 4-inch and Hedgehog A/S mortars and depth charges), and with an endurance of 7,200 miles at 12 knots. The early ships were also fitted for minesweeping. ANNAN, completed in June 1944, was manned by the Royal Canadian Navy. She worked up and then joined the Sixth Escort Group. Her service took her from Londonderry to Iceland and the Azores. On 16 October 1944 she sank U-1006 whilst on A/S Patrol south of the Faeroes. For her last two months war service her group operated out of Halifax, Nova Scotia. In June 1945 she paid off, and was handed back to the Royal Navy. In November 1945 she was sold to the Royal Danish Navy and renamed NIELS EBBE-SEN. She was broken up in 1963.

ANTELOPE

The destroyer ANTELOPE is seen here at speed. One of the first destroyers built for the RN after the Great War, she was completed in 1930. In 1939 she was part of the Home Fleet. On 5 February 1940 she attacked and sank U-41 in the S.W. Approaches, the first occasion in the war of a single escort sinking a submerged U-boat. In April 1940 she was damaged in a collision during the Norwegian Campaign. After repairs she took part in the Dakar Expedition, escorting home the cruiser FIJI which had been torpedoed. While on Atlantic escort duties on 2 November 1940 she sank U-31, rescuing 43 of her crew. She re-joined the Home Fleet, escorting a minelayer and then the ill-fated HOOD and PRINCE OF WALES, taking part in the search for HOOD's survivors. In August 1941 she took part in a raid on Spitzbergen. She helped cover the passage of carriers taking aircraft to Malta, and also the Harpoon Malta convoy, during which she towed the damaged cruiser LIVERPOOL back to Gibraltar. In August she took part in the Pedestal convoy to Malta, then joined the South Atlantic Station before taking part in the North African landings and convoys. In August 1944 she was placed in reserve before being broken up in 1946.

ARBITER (25 February 1945)

The ARBITER was a trade escort carrier built at Seattle, America under a Lease-Lend Agreement. Of 11,420 tons, she was armed with two 5-inch guns and 47 smaller AA weapons. She completed in December 1943. After alterations in Vancouver, she passed through the Panama Canal in April, embarked aircraft at New York and arrived off the Clyde in June 1944. She carried out two trips to America to ferry aircraft to Britain and then refitted prior to working up in the East Indies. She arrived at Trincomalee in April 1945 and sailed on to join the British Pacific Fleet. In June she was allocated to the Air Train, part of the Fleet Train. Her task was to serve as a ferry and replenishment carrier, operating forward from the base at Manus. ARBITER carried out two replenishment operations and was used on occasions as an auxiliary oiler. After the surrender of Japan she returned to Sydney and was used for deck landing training. In October she called at Hong Kong returning to Sydney with Allied prisoners of war. She sailed for the UK at the end of 1945 and was returned to the USN in March 1946. She was taken into mercantile service as MV CORACERO, before being broken up in 1972.

ARGONAUT

The cruiser ARGONAUT is seen here heading across the Atlantic to Philadelphia for repairs after she had been torpedoed forward and aft in the Mediterranean. Completed in August 1942, two months later she carried out a special trip to North Russia taking aid for British sick and wounded, returning with survivors from earlier convoys. She then sailed south for the North African landings. Afterwards she joined the cruisers AURORA and SIRIUS to form a very effective striking force base on Bone. Whilst returning from one of these sweeps at 25 knots she was torpedoed by the Italian Submarine MOCENIGO, losing her bow and stern. She was able to proceed slowly and help fight off air attacks. After temporary repairs she crossed the Atlantic to Philadelphia, steering by main engines. Her repairs there, and later in the UK, lasted to March 1944. She took part in the Normandy landings, firing 4395 shells in 25 days. In August 1944 she took part in the landings in the South of France, and then operated in the Aegean. She later joined the East Indies Fleet, supporting strikes on Sumatra. She went on to join the British Pacific Fleet and took part in the operations off Okinawa. She returned to the UK in June 1946, being placed in reserve. She was broken up in 1955.

9

AURORA (30 October 1943)

The cruiser AURORA was badly damaged by a 500-Kg. bomb on 30 October 1943 whilst operating in the Aegean. She was seriously damaged but made harbour under her own power. She had been completed in 1937. When war broke out she patrolled the Norwegian coast. In April 1940 she took part in the Norwegian campaign, being damaged by a bomb on 7 May. She took part in the search for the BISMARCK in May 1941 and in June helped sink the German tanker BELCHEN in the North Atlantic. She carried out a raid on Spitzbergen, later helping to sink the German BREMSE. In October 1941 she joined a very successful striking force operating out of Malta. AURORA was known as "The Silver Phantom". In December the force ran into a minefield, and had to be disbanded. Repairs in Malta under air attacks took till March. She joined the Home Fleet in July and in November took part in the North Africa landings, helping to destroy 2 French destroyers. She then joined a striking force operating off North Africa, covering the landings in Sicily and Italy, before being damaged in the Aegean. Repairs took till April 1944. She took part in the South of France landings and then returned to the Aegean. In 1946 she was refitted prior to transferring to the Chinese Nationalist Navy as the CHUNGKING. She became a hulk in 1955.

BAMBOROUGH CASTLE

Another of the very successful Castle class corvettes, BAMBOROUGH CASTLE was completed at Aberdeen on 30 May 1944. These ships were a continuation of the successful Flower Class corvette design, using the expertise of shipyards whose slips were too small to build the new frigates. They were limited in performance by their single propeller, having a speed of 16.5 knots. She worked up in June/July 1944 at Tobermory then joined the Western Approaches Command as part of Group B5, escorting convoys. In October she transferred to Group B7 and on 9 December 1944 sank U-387. She escorted Russian convoys in November 1944 to April 1945, when she was laid up at Sheerness. She was commissioned for Fishery protection duties from January to September 1946. She was then placed in reserve at Devonport and later at Penarth before being broken up in 1959.

BARHAM

The battleship BARHAM had served in the Great War, and damaged during the Battle of Jutland. She underwent major refits between the wars, but did not receive the massive up-dating to her armament and machinery that three of her sisters were given. At the outbreak of war she was in the Mediterranean and was sent to join the Home Fleet to cover Atlantic Convoys against raiders. On 12 December 1939 she rammed and sank the destroyer DUCHESS in fog, and on 28th she was torpedoed by U-30 off the Hebrides. Repairs took six months. Afterwards she joined the operation against Dakar, carrying out bombardments. She towed the damaged battleship RESOLUTION back from Dakar. After operations with Force H off Gibraltar, she re-joined the Mediterranean Fleet and supported operations in the desert, bombarding Sollum and Bardia. In March she took part in the Battle of Cape Matapan when 3 Italian cruisers were sunk. In April she bombarded Tripoli and the next month she took part in Operations off Crete, when she was damaged by air attacks - repairs taking till July. In November, whilst operating with the Fleet off the Egyptian coast, she was torpedoed by U-331 and capsized after 5 minutes. 862 of her crew were lost.

BETONY

The BETONY was a modified Flower Class corvette, with a longer endurance, of 7,400 miles at 10 knots, than earlier ships of the class. She was of 980 tons and was fitted with radar on her bridge. She was armed with a single 4-inch and three 20-mm guns. She was completed at Aberdeen in August 1943. After work up she was allocated to the East Indies, and, after escorting convoys on her way through the Mediterranean, arrived at Colombo in January 1944. She then carried out convoy escort duties in the Indian Ocean and refitted in Durban in February 1945. In March 1945 she was transferred to the Royal Indian Navy as the SIND, remaining on the East Indies Station. She paid off in January 1946 and in March 1947 became the Royal Thai Ship PRASAE. She ran aground on 13 January 1951 while carrying out a bombardment during the Korean War, and had to be destroyed.

BLACKMORE

The escort destroyer BLACKMORE was in the second group of the Hunt Class escort destroyers. She was armed with three twin 4-inch guns and had a speed of 27 knots. She completed in April 1942, being allocated to the Eastern Fleet. She sailed from the UK for Freetown in June 1942.and undertook escort duties off the Cape and East Africa. She was temporarily transferred to the South Atlantic Escort Force for a short period. After a spell off West Africa she joined the Mediterranean Fleet in August 1943. She took part in the Salerno landings in September 1943, coming under fire from shore batteries. In January 1944 she took part in the Anzio landings, carrying out bombardments. In June 1944 she was in action with four E-boats off the Yugoslav coast, sinking one. She later took part in the South of France landings, and in October 1944 returned to the UK to join the Nore Command. In March 1945 she sailed for the Far East via the Mediterranean, and acted as a weather reporting ship for the relief of Rangoon. She left Singapore for the UK in October 1945, and was placed in reserve at Devonport. In 1952 she was transferred to the Royal Danish Navy and renamed ESBERN SNARE. She was sold in 1966.

BLACK PRINCE

The BLACK PRINCE was a modified Dido Class cruiser completed in November 1943. These ships carried only four, not five, twin 5.25-inch guns, and had vertical masts and funnels with altogether a lower profile. She operated against blockade-runners in the Bay of Biscay and in February 1944 took part in Arctic convoys. In April 1944 she was in action with German destroyers in the Channel, one destroyer being sunk. During the Normandy landings she was with the Western (US) Task Force, coming under fire from ashore. In August 1944 she took part in the landings in the South of France and then served in the Aegean carrying out bombardments and in operations against enemy shipping. In October 1944 she was at Athens helping to restore law and order . She then went on to operate with the East Indies Fleet against Sumatra. She joined the British Pacific Fleet in March 1945 and took part in Operations off Okinawa and then the Sakishima-Gunto Group. In July she shelled the Hitachi area of Honshu. She was lent to the Royal New Zealand Navy in 1946 and was at the Coronation Review in 1953. Paid off in 1960, she was broken up in 1962.

BLUEBELL

The corvette BLUEBELL was typical of the many Flower Class corvettes built for the Navy on a design by Smith's Docks. She completed in July 1940 and immediately joined the Western Approaches, Northern Escort Forces escorting convoys. Much of her early duties included searching for U-boats and rescuing survivors from sunken ships. In October 1940 she reported she was carrying 203 survivors from 5 ships. She escorted convoys as far south as Gibraltar and in December 1941 she sighted and attacked U-67 on the surface but was only able to cause slight damage. After a refit during which her forecastle was extended aft and fitted with the Hedgehog A/S mortar, she escorted a convoy to Russia, which lost 13 out of 40 ships. She returned to the Western Approaches, but also escorted further Russian convoys and operated in the Kola Inlet. In July 1943 she escorted assault convoys to Bone ready for the invasion of Sicily. She then escorted convoys in the Mediterranean before returning to Western Approaches in December. Afterwards she carried out more Russian convoys and also escorted LSTs for Normandy. During convoy RA 64, a return convoy from Russia, she was torpedoed by U-711 on 17 February 1945 and blew up. There was only 1 survivor.

BOXER

The BOXER was one of three Landing Ship Tanks (1) built by Harland and Wolff. She was driven by steam turbines and had a speed of 17 knots. Her funnel was offset to starboard to clear the tank deck. She could carry 13 x 30-ton tanks, 27 x 3-ton lorries and 193 troops. These were the first ships built as LSTs. Completed in May 1943 she sailed at once for Gibraltar and was in the assault convoys for the Sicily invasion. She then went to Malta before taking part in the Salerno landings in September. In January 1944 she took part in the Anzio landings. In February she was heavily damaged in a gale when she was driven ashore off Naples. After temporary repairs she sailed for UK and refitted as a Fighter Direction Ship, completing in June 1945. She was allocated to the East Indies Station, but only reached Malta before the war ended. She returned to the UK and was used as a radar training ship, when she became the only four masted ship in the RN. She was placed in reserve in 1955, being used as an accommodation ship, and was handed over for breaking up in 1958.

BRAZEN

The destroyer BRAZEN was completed in April 1931. She was one of the standard pre-war destroyers armed with four 4.7-inch guns and carrying eight torpedo tubes. She had a designed speed of 35.25 knots, and reached 35.38 on trials. In September 1939 she was in the Dover Command and took part in several U-boat searches. In February 1940 she joined the Home Fleet, and again took part in U-boat hunts and was close by when the destroyer DARING was torpedoed and sunk. In April 1940 whilst escorting a convoy to Norway, she and FEARLESS sank U-49. She then screened heavy ships and escorted other convoys in the area. In May 1940 she rammed a wreck off the Wash and had to be repaired but was escorting convoys between Dover and Folkestone again in July. The convoys came under heavy air attacks, and whilst helping to fight off attacks round convoy CW7 on 20 July she was badly damaged by near misses which broke her back. She was then hit in the engine room and sank. Only 1 of her crew was lost.

(G.M. Hudson Collection)

BRIDLINGTON (28 November 1941)

The minesweeper BRIDLINGTON was a Bangor Class vessel built by Denny and completed in October 1940. She was one of the diesel-engined ships of the class, and was shorter than her steam driven sisters, which needed extra length for a boiler room. She was armed with a 3-inch AA gun forward and four machine guns. Her engines could drive her at 16 knots. Initially she joined the 9th Minesweeping Flotilla at Scapa Flow. Later she served on the East Coast and in the Channel, operating from Portsmouth, Portland and Harwich. In August 1942 she escorted vessels on the Dieppe raid and in June 1944 she took part in the Normandy landings, sweeping the route to Juno Beach on D-Day. She was put in reserve in the Tees in June 1945. In 1946 she was transferred to the Air Ministry before being broken up at Plymouth in 1960.

CAISTOR CASTLE (25 January 1945)

The corvette CAISTOR CASTLE was completed in September 1944. These ships were designed by Smith's Dock, who had also designed the Flower Class corvettes. Five of the class were completed as rescue ships. After working up at Tobermory she joined the 30th Escort Group working out of Londonderry, carrying out patrols and escorting convoys. In July 1945 she was at Gibraltar on Search and Air Rescue duties until November 1945, when she continued those duties off Freetown. She visited Bermuda in January 1946 and then returned to Devonport via New York. In May 1946 she was put in reserve. Refitted in 1949, she represented the Reserve Fleet at the Coronation Review in 1953. She commissioned for the Second Frigate squadron at Portland on training duties from 1953-55. She was then laid up again, before being broken up in 1956.

CALDER

The CALDER was one of the Captain Class destroyer escorts built in the United States for the Royal Navy. CALDER was of the turbo-electric group of the class, long hulled compared to her diesel electric propelled half sisters, with a speed of 24 knots and a main gunnery armament of three 3-inch guns. She was unusual in mounting a twin 40-mm gun in X-position. One of her class was completed in less than two months, the average building time being 6 months. CALDER commissioned in July 1943. She joined the Fourth Escort group, the first composed entirely of Captain Class ships, operating in the North Atlantic. From November 1943 to October 1944 the Group escorted large troop ships between UK and Naples. The Group then returned to duty in the Western Approaches, where, on 26 January 1945, CALDER helped sink U-1051. On 8 April 1945 she helped sink U-744 south west of Cape Clear. In May she arrived at Belfast for conversion to a Coastal Forces Control frigate ready for the East Indies, but the war ended before she was deployed. She was returned to the United States Navy in October 1945.

K349

CHARYBDIS (October 1943)

The Dido Class cruisers were built to provide anti-aircraft cover for the Fleet, being armed with five twin 5.25-inch guns. However, production difficulties arose, and two, SCYLLA and CHARYBDIS, were completed with four twin 4.5-inch gun instead. Built by Cammell Lairds, she completed in December 1941. After trials and work up she joined the Home Fleet, covering minelaying operations. In April 1942 she joined the North Atlantic Command and covered reinforcements for Malta. In the autumn she operated in the North Atlantic searching for blockade-runners and in October again covered aircraft reinforcements for Malta. In November 1942 she joined Force H and carried the Allied Force HQ for Operation Torch to Algiers. The next month she rejoined the Home Fleet and patrolled the North Sea, covering minelaying operations and later covering convoys in the Bay of Biscay. In August 1943 she escorted convoys in the Mediterranean and took part in the Salerno landings. She returned to the Bay of Biscay patrols. On 23 October 1943 she was torpedoed off the Channel Islands by German destroyers and was lost with 462 lives.

COTSWOLD (31 October 1941)

COTSWOLD was an escort destroyer of the Hunt Class. She joined the 16th Flotilla operating out of Harwich on completion in November 1940, covering East Coast convoys. The 2-pounder gun fitted on her bow was to contend with E-boats. In March 1941 she was in collision with the trawler ST DONATS and on 20 April 1942 was mined off Orfordness, losing four of her crew. She was towed to Chatham for repairs, which lasted to May 1943. On 24 October 1943 she was again badly damaged in collision with the destroyer MONTROSE. Repairs took until May 1944. She took part in the Normandy landings being part of the Eastern Task Force escorting convoys. On 8 September 1944 she was in collision with the SS CHIGNECTO PARK. On the night of 14-15 January 1945 she was in action with E-boats. After a refit from November 1945 to March 1946 she was placed in reserve where she remained until being broken up in 1957.

COVENTRY (20 June 1940)

COVENTRY was built as a light cruiser and completed in 1918 with five 6-inch guns. In 1935 she was refitted and emerged as a prototype AA cruiser armed with a main armament of ten single 4-inch AA guns. She was in the Mediterranean from 1937 to October 1939, when she was recalled to home waters. She was damaged by near misses during the Norwegian campaign. In August she returned to the Mediterranean to cover convoys in the Red Sea, and Eastern Mediterranean. She was damaged by a torpedo from the Italian submarine NEGHELLI in December 1940. She continued operating despite having no bow below her waterline. In April she took part in the evacuation of Greece, and the next month was damaged by a near miss off Crete. Repairs had to wait until October 1941, meanwhile she remained operational. After repairs in Bombay she returned to the Mediterranean and took part in Operation Vigorous, an unsuccessful attempt to run a convoy to Malta from the East. She was lost on 14 September 1942 whilst trying to cover the destroyers ZULU and SIKH during an assault on Tobruk. She was attacked by 15 Stuka aircraft and hit by four large bombs, machine gun and cannon fire. She had to be sunk by ZULU. She lost 64 of her crew.

DEVONSHIRE

The DEVONSHIRE was a County Class cruiser armed with four twin 8-inch guns and completed at Devonport in March 1929. When war was declared she was in the Mediterranean, but returned to the Home Fleet in November 1939. She took part in the evacuation of Norway, being slightly damaged by near misses. In June she brought the King of Norway to Britain. She took part in the Dakar operation and patrolled the South Atlantic for raiders and escorted convoys. In August she went north to cover Russian convoys. In October 1941 she returned to the South Atlantic and on 22 November sank the German raider ATLANTIS. In April 1942 she took part in the Madagascar operation and then served in the Eastern Fleet. She rejoined the Home Fleet after a refit in April 1944, and covered operations on the Norwegian coast against TIRPITZ and other shipping. In May 1945 she took part in the occupation of Norway. Afterwards she escorted the King of Norway back to Oslo. After a period of trooping duties, she was partly disarmed and was employed as the Cadets' Training Ship from May 1947 to September 1953. She was then placed in reserve and broken up in 1954.

DIANELLA (22 April 1942)

A Flower Class corvette, DIANELLA was originally to have been named DAFFODIL. She completed in January 1941, one of a large class designed to produce a large number of convoy escorts rapidly at the outbreak of war. After work up she joined the First Escort Group operating out of Londonderry, escorting convoys, rescuing survivors and attacking U-boats. In 1942 she was fitted with radar, and also carried out trials on 18-inch depth charge mortars. Two were fitted each side of A gun (see photograph). Afterwards she returned to her Atlantic convoy duties. In June 1942 she transferred to Arctic Convoys, escorting convoy PQ 17, which had to scatter when threatened by German heavy surface forces. She helped bring the surviving ships to Archangel after attacks by submarines and aircraft. She then helped cover convoys for the N. African landings. During a refit in December 1942 she was fitted with the Hedgehog ahead throwing A/S weapon. In July she covered an assault convoy for the invasion of Sicily, remaining in the Mediterranean till October. She then escorted further Russian convoys prior to taking part in the Normandy landings. After further service in the North Atlantic, she was laid up in June 1945 and was broken up 3 years later.

EAGLE

The aircraft carrier EAGLE was originally laid down as the Chilean battleship ALMIRANTE COCHRANE in 1913. Purchased by the Admiralty in 1917, she was completed as an aircraft carrier, being launched in June 1918 and started trials in April 1920. She was then taken to Portsmouth for further work and finally commissioned in February 1924. She introduced the "island" and double story hangar in aircraft carrier design. She served on the Mediterranean Station and in the Far East. She was on the China Station when war broke out. She carried out searches for raiders and escorted troop convoys. Later she returned via the Red Sea, and took part in operations in the Mediterranean. She took part in no less than nine operations to ferry 183 fighters to Malta. In August 1942 she took part in the Pedestal convoy to Malta. On 11 August, whilst with the convoy, she was hit by four torpedoes from U-73 and sank in under 8 minutes. There were 927 survivors and four of her Sea Hurricanes which were airborne at the time were able to land on the other carriers.

EDINBURGH

The cruiser EDINBURGH was completed less than a month before the war began. She was armed with four triple 6-inch turrets, and was larger than her half sisters of the Southampton Class, being 22 feet longer and two feet beamier. When the war began she was used on patrols between Iceland and the Faeroes, and then transferred to the Humber Force. She suffered minor damage from a near miss during air attacks in the Firth of Forth in October 1939. She covered convoys and the raid on the Lofoten Islands in March 1941. She also carried out patrols in the Denmark Strait. She entered the Mediterranean to cover convoys to Malta in July 41 (Substance) and September (Halberd). In December 1941 she escorted Russian convoys, and on 30 April 1942, whilst covering return convoy QP11 her stern was blown off by torpedoes fired by U-456. She was taken in tow bound for Murmansk, but later managed to proceed slowly under her own power. On 2 May she came under air attack, and then encountered 3 German destroyers, one of which she hit and disabled. She was again torpedoed, and had to be abandoned and sunk. 58 of her crew were lost. Gold bars she was carrying were recovered by divers in 1981.

EMERALD

The cruiser EMERALD was launched on the Tyne in 1920 and completed at Chatham in 1925. She was armed with seven 6-inch guns and 12 (later 16) torpedo tubes. She achieved 32.9 knots on trials. Most of her pre-war service was spent on the East Indies Station. She had re-commissioned in July 1939 and joined the Northern Patrol. In October 1939 she took gold bullion to Canada and then covered convoys in the Atlantic, shipping more bullion in December. In September 1940 she joined the Western Approaches Command and in October accompanied the battleship REVENGE on a bombardment of Cherbourg. A few days later she and the cruiser NEWCASTLE engaged four German destroyers at long range in a chase that reached 32.5 knots at one point. She then escorted convoys to Capetown, helped in the occupation of E. African ports, and in March 1942 was with the Eastern Fleet during the Japanese advance into the Indian Ocean. In July 1942 she underwent modernisation in the UK before returning to the East Indies. She returned to the UK for the Normandy landings, where she was in the bombardment forces. She was damaged in an air attack. After repairs, she was placed in reserve and was then used for trials before being broken up in 1948.

EMPEROR

The EMPEROR (ex USS PYBUS) was an assault escort carrier built in Seattle and commissioned in New York City in August 1943. Of 11,200 tons, she carried up to 30 aircraft for operations but could ferry 90. She was allocated to the Western Approaches Command and worked up in the Clyde in September. In March 1944 she joined the Home Fleet and took part in Operation Tungsten, a strike on the battleship TIRPITZ. In May she returned to the Western Approaches for convoy escort duties and in July 1944 transferred to the Mediterranean, taking part in the South of France landings in August. In September she covered operations off Greece and in the Aegean, flying 1500 sorties before returning to the UK. In March 1945 she sailed for the East Indies and in April 1945 her aircraft carried out a reconnaissance of the Port Swettenham area and strikes on Rangoon. In July her aircraft struck at Car Nicobar and in September took part in the occupation of Singapore. She returned to the UK in December 1945 and in January sailed to the USA to be returned to the USN in February 1946.

EMPIRE MACCOLL

The oiler EMPIRE MACCOLL was converted to carry aircraft, as well as her cargo, whilst under construction at Birkenhead. She carried three Swordfish aircraft on her flight deck, which was fitted over her oil tanks, and had no hangar. The aircraft used the after 100 ft. of the flight deck as a park. She was also armed with a 4-inch gun and eight Oerlikons. She had a speed of 11 knots. As a mercantile aircraft carrier the weight of her cargo gave her more stability for aircraft operations than the lighter laden escort carriers. She completed in November 1943 and was employed on North Atlantic convoys to May 1945. Later that year the flight deck was removed and in 1946 she was renamed BRITISH PILOT and was used commercially by British Petroleum, for whom she had been building in 1943. She was broken up in 1962.

ESCAPADE (12 February 1945)

The destroyer ESCAPADE had been completed in 1934 and at the outbreak of war was employed on convoy escort duties. In February 1940 she was escorting a convoy when U-63 was sighted astern and attacked. ESCAPADE rescued the crew. She took part in the Norwegian campaign and in June was transferred to the newly formed Force H at Gibraltar. She took part in the Dakar operation and later escorted Russian convoys. She also covered the attempted withdrawal of the damaged cruiser TRINIDAD. In June 1942 she escorted the Harpoon convoy to Malta before returning to Russian convoys and later escorted convoys for the invasion of North Africa. In December 1942 she joined Escort Group B3 of the Western Approaches Command. In September 1943 she was badly damaged by an explosion onboard when attacking a U-boat. Repairs took until December 1944, when she rejoined the Western Approaches Command, being fitted with the new Squid anti-submarine mortar for trials (seen here in A position). In June 1945 she escorted Norwegian ships back to Norway and then joined the Anti-Submarine Training Flotilla. She paid off in November 1946 and was handed over for breaking up in 1947.

EURYALUS (9 October 1941)

The light cruiser EURYALUS was completed in June 1941. She escorted the Halberd convoy to Malta in September 1941. She then sailed via the Cape to Alexandria to join the Mediterranean Fleet. She supported troop operations with bombardments and escorting troopships. She also escorted convoys to Malta, taking part in the Second Battle of Sirte in March 1942, when she and other light cruisers and destroyers drove off an Italian battleship and heavy cruisers from a convoy. She also took part in an abortive attempt to sail a convoy from Alexandria in June 1942. In November she escorted the first convoy to Malta after the siege had been raised. She then joined a cruiser striking force based on Malta. After supporting landings in Sicily and Salerno, she returned to the UK for a refit in October 1943, having not sustained any damage despite being in the fiercest fighting. After a spell operating off the Norwegian coast, she sailed for operations against Japan, covering strikes against Sumatra before joining the British Pacific Fleet. She took part in operations against the Ryukyu Islands and the mainland of Japan. She was at the relief of Hong Kong in August 1945. She returned to the UK in 1947, was placed in reserve in 1954,. and was broken up in 1959.

EXETER (1941)

The cruiser EXETER was built at Devonport Dockyard, completing in July 1931. Armed with three twin 8-inch guns, she was a development of the County Class, and the last of the British heavy cruiser types. She had just paid off when war was imminent, and her crew was recalled on 23 August 1939. She sailed for the South Atlantic, where she guarded shipping and searched for raiders. On 13 December 1939, she, and the AJAX and ACHILLES, met and engaged the pocket battleship GRAF SPEE. EXETER was severely mauled, and lost 61 of her crew and had to retire to the Falklands. She returned to Devonport for repairs and sailed in March 1941 before completion due to the intensity of local air raids. She escorted convoys in the Atlantic and to the Cape and Indian Ocean. In February 1942 she joined the Allied striking Force in the Java Sea, and took part in the Battle of Java Sea. She was damaged by an enemy shell, which wrecked a boiler room. She had to retire to Sourabaya for repairs, sailing the following day for Trincomalee. After 12 hours steaming, she and her two destroyer escorts encountered a vastly superior force of Japanese warships, and all 3 were sunk. She lost 54 of her crew in the action, whilst the remainder were taken captive.

FAULKNOR (27 August 1942)

The FAULKNOR was Leader of the F Class Destroyer Flotilla. In 1939 she was in the Home Fleet and a few days after war broke out, on 14 September, whilst escorting the carrier ARK ROYAL, she helped sink U-39. She escorted troop convoys across the Atlantic and in March 1940 was present when U-44 was sunk. In April 1940 she was in action off Narvik, and in June joined the newly formed Force H at Gibraltar. In April 1941 she escorted the ARK ROYAL on two trips to fly aircraft to Malta. In May she escorted convoys in the Mediterranean and later that month sailed with Force H to the Atlantic to engage the BISMARCK. On 18 June she helped sink U-138 off Cape St Vincent. The next month she took part in the Substance convoy to Malta. In December 1941 she escorted the battleship DUKE OF YORK to the USA. On 12 September 1942 she sank U-88 while on Russian convoys. During these convoys she came under air attack and suffered severe weather conditions. In 1943 she took part the invasions of Sicily and Italy. In September she moved to the Aegean, supporting troops ashore and carrying out bombardments. She returned to UK in May 1944 and escorted convoys to the Normandy landings. In June 1945 she carried the King and Queen to the Channel Islands. She was then placed in reserve before being broken up in 1946.

FERNIE

The FERNIE was an escort destroyer of the first Hunt class. She was completed in May 1940, and like her sisters, was armed with two twin 4-inch guns, stability problems precluding the fitting of a third mounting. She was later fitted with a 2-pounder bow chaser for use against E-boats. She joined the Home Fleet and in June 1940 took part in the evacuations from Le Havre and Cherbourg. In August she transferred to the Portsmouth Command and then covered convoys in the Channel and on the West Coast. In February 1942 she operated in the Channel searching for the SCHARNHORST and GNEISENAU after their escape from Brest, and later continued convoy escort duties. In August 1942 took part in the raid on Dieppe. In December 1942 she joined the Nore Command and in June 1944 was in the Eastern Task Force escorting convoys to Normandy and then remained in the Channel on patrol until November. She then returned to Sheerness. In June 1945 she visited Wilhelmshaven and in August 1945 she became an aircraft target ship until she paid off in 1948. She was broken up in November 1956.

FIREDRAKE

The destroyer FIREDRAKE was completed in 1935. On 11 September 1939 she helped sink U-39 which had attacked the ARK ROYAL. In March she operated off Norway and carried out further searches for U-boats. During the Norwegian campaign she escorted convoys; carried out bombardments; and helped withdraw troops, suffering minor damage from air attacks in the process. Afterwards she covered convoys and minelaying operations, and in August 1940 helped pass reinforcements to the Eastern Mediterranean. She joined Force H in September 1940. On 18 October 1940 she helped sink the Italian submarine DUBBO east of Gibraltar. In November she escorted a convoy to Malta. In March 1941 she grounded off Gibraltar in fog. She was repaired at Gibraltar and Chatham, before rejoining Force H in July. Later that month she took part in the Substance convoy to Malta, being badly damaged by a near miss, and had to return to Gibraltar. Repairs were carried out at Gibraltar and the USA. She joined the Western Approaches forces in January 1942, and joined Escort Group B7 in May 1942. In December 1942 the convoy she was escorting came under heavy attack. FIREDRAKE was torpedoed on the 16th by U-211 and broke in two, her forward end sinking at once but her stern remained afloat until the next day.

GALATEA

The cruiser GALATEA was armed with three twin 6-inch guns. She completed in August 1935, and in September 1939 was Flagship of the Mediterranean Destroyers. In March 1940 she was recalled to the Home Fleet and carried out sweeps of the Skagerrak. During the Norwegian campaign she was bombed several times but not damaged. In May she escorted ships with bullion from Holland to Southend. Later that month she bombarded Calais and covered the evacuation of Dunkirk. She was damaged by a mine in September and subsequent repairs took till January 1941. She then rejoined the Home Fleet, carrying out sweeps, patrols and covering minelaying operations. She took part in the hunt for the BISMARCK. She joined the Mediterranean Fleet via the Cape, arriving in mid August 1941. She supported the relief of Tobruk in August and the next month operated in the Red Sea. She carried out bombardments near Tobruk to support the Army in October. In November she escorted troopships. She was returning from an operation in the Central Mediterranean on 14 December 1941 when she was torpedoed and sunk by U-557. She lost 470 of her crew.

GANNET
The GANNET was a river gunboat launched and delivered in November 1927 by Yarrows. Of 310 tons, she was armed with two single 3-inch AA guns, one forward and one aft, and eight machine guns. She had steam turbines giving her a speed of 16 knots. She commissioned in March 1928 at Hong Kong for duty on the China Station on the Yangtse River. She was damaged by Japanese aircraft during the Sino-Japanese War. In December 1939 she was placed in reserve at Chung King and half her crew were sent back to Britain by rail. Her hull, together with those of the gunboats FALCON and SANDPIPER, was presented to the Chinese Government on 13 February 1942 and she was renamed YING SHAN (BRITISH MOUNTAIN) and survived to the 1960s.

GLASGOW

The cruiser GLASGOW was completed in 1937. She was at Scapa Flow when war was declared. In April she was preparing to embark troops when the Germans invaded Norway. During the Norwegian campaign she landed seamen and marines and was damaged in air attacks. She helped evacuate Aandalsnes, and took the King of Norway to Tromso. On 17 July 1940 she collided with the destroyer IMOGEN, which exploded and sank. Repairs took until October. In November she joined the Mediterranean Fleet and covered convoys to Malta. In December 1940 she was hit by two aircraft torpedoes while at Crete, but was able to reach Alexandria under her own power. After temporary repairs she operated in the Indian Ocean and in May 1942 sailed for a refit at New York, which lasted till August. In March 1943 she intercepted the blockade-runner REGENSBURG. In December she and the cruiser ENTERPRISE encountered 5 German destroyers accompanied by 6 torpedo boats. The cruisers chased the Germans, sinking three. During the Normandy landings she was hit by shore batteries. After repairs she sailed for the Far East, arriving at Colombo after VJ Day. She finally paid off in 1956 and was handed over for breaking up in 1958.

GRAFTON

The destroyer GRAFTON completed in March 1936 and was in the Mediterranean when war broke out. She transferred to the Western Approaches Command in October and carried out patrols and escort duty. In January she transferred to Harwich, intercepting shipping off the Dutch coast. In April she took part in the Norwegian campaign and in late May took part in a bombardment of Calais. She then took part in the evacuation from Dunkirk. She lifted troops from La Panne and Braye, landing 860 men at Dover on 27 May. Early in the morning of 29 May, the destroyer WAKEFUL, carrying soldiers from Dunkirk, was torpedoed and GRAFTON stopped nearby to rescue survivors. GRAFTON was then torpedoed by U-62. A second explosion occurred, and in the confusion she was then rammed by the minesweeper LYDD. Her crew and soldiers abandoned ship, being rescued by the IVANHOE and MALINES. The IVANHOE sank the wreck by gunfire. 15 of her crew were lost.

GRAMPUS

The GRAMPUS was a Porpoise class minelaying submarine of 1,520 tons. She was armed with a single 4-inch gun and six bow torpedo tubes and could carry 50 mines. She had a surface speed of 15.75 knots, and a submerged speed of 8.75 knots. Six of the class were built, and three were cancelled. She was built at Chatham Dockyard, completing in March 1937. She sailed for the China Station in 1937 and was there when war broke out. In May 1940 she was recalled to the Mediterranean Station. She sailed from Malta on 10 June 1940 to lay mines in the Channel off Augusta. She became overdue and it was later discovered that she had been sunk by the Italian torpedo boats CLIO and CIRCE in depth charge attacks off Syracuse on the evening of 16 June. There were no survivors.

GRASSHOLM

The Isles Class Trawler was built for anti-submarine and minesweeping operations. Of 545 tons, she was armed with a 12-pounder gun forward and three Oerlikons, as well as with depth charges in rails and on throwers. She had a speed of 12.25 knots. She was built by John Lewis and Sons, Aberdeen, completing in August 1943. She joined the 31st Trawler Group operating in the Plymouth Command, escorting convoys in the Channel. After the Normandy landings, she transferred to the Nore Command, and operated out of Sheerness, and later from Ostend. She paid off to reserve in July 1945 and sold to a Norwegian company for commercial use in April 1946, retaining her original name.

HARDY

The destroyer HARDY was the second ship of her name in the War, the first having been lost during the First Battle of Narvik in April 1940. This vessel was the leader of the V Class of Emergency War Design destroyers, and was completed on the Clyde in August 1943. After work up she joined the Home Fleet and carried out anti-U-boat patrols and escort duties. On 22 November 1943 she sailed for Seidisfjord with a Russian convoy. She undertook further Russian convoy escort duties, and on 30 January 1944, whilst escorting convoy JW 56B, was hit by a homing torpedo fired by U-278 about 60 miles south of Bear Island. She had to be sunk by torpedoes from her Flotilla mate VENUS. 40 of her crew were lost.

HAWKINS (June 1942)

The cruiser HAWKINS was completed in July 1919 with a heavy armament of seven 7.5-inch guns to counter German light cruisers. She had a good speed (29.5 knots) and radius of action and was designed with two sets of boilers so that she could use either coal or fuel oil. The coal-fired boilers were removed in 1928. In the 1930s she was demilitarised (with only four 4-inch and four 2-pounder guns) and used as a boy's training ship. At the outbreak of war she was in the Reserve Fleet and was re-armed with seven 7.5-inch and four 4-inch guns. She joined the South Atlantic Station in early 1940 for escort duties and to search for raiders. In 1941 she helped capture ports in East Africa and also captured Axis merchant ships. She was refitted in UK in late 1941 before joining the Eastern Fleet for escort duties. In March 1944 she returned to the UK and was part of the bombarding force for the Normandy landings in the American sector. After a refit she became a training ship again. She was placed in reserve in June 1945. She was then used for bombing trials, when only 29 hits were obtained out of 616 bombs dropped on her whilst at anchor. She was handed over for breaking up in 1947.

HELFORD

The River Class frigate HELFORD was built at Aberdeen, completing in June 1943, just one year after being laid down. She was armed with two single 4-inch guns, four (later increased to ten) Oerlikons, a Hedgehog anti-submarine mortar and depth charges. She joined the Third Escort group based on Londonderry and in August 1943 transferred to the South Atlantic Escort Force. In November she took part in the operation to stop a Japanese blockade running submarine. In January 1944 she joined the Eastern Fleet, escorting convoys between Aden and Bombay. In November 1945 she left Aden for the UK and reduced to reserve in March 1946. She remained in reserve at Devonport, and later Lisahally, until she was broken up in 1956.

HERMES

HERMES was the first ship in the world designed and built as an aircraft carrier. She was completed in 1924. She had two propellers and could steam at 25 knots. She had a hangar aft from which aircraft could be transferred to the flight deck by an electrical lift sited on her quarterdeck. She served on the China and Mediterranean Stations before the War. She proved to be a steady ship at sea and had a good size flight deck. When war was declared she covered the movement of the BEF to France, and searched for raiders in the Atlantic. She was used on convoy escort duties and supported troops in operations against Italian East Africa, and helped prevent German intervention in Iraq. In January 1942 she was attached to the Australian squadron but the next month returned to the East Indies. In April 1942 she was sent to Trincomalee to prepare for the assault on Madagascar. When the Japanese advance towards Ceylon became known she was sailed from Trincomalee harbour, but was sighted and was attacked by 50 Japanese aircraft off Ceylon on the 9th. She was hit by 40 bombs and was sunk. 600 survivors were rescued by a nearby hospital ship, but 307 of her crew were lost.

HIGHWAY (November 1943)

Early trials with Landing Ships Tank (LSTs) were disappointing, and so Landing Ships Dock (LSDs) were developed to carry laden LCTs (Landing Craft Tanks) close to the assault beaches. There, they would flood their dock and launch the landing craft. However, LSTs were later developed successfully. Nevertheless, four of these ships were built for the Royal Navy, and 13 for the USN, and proved the forerunners for the very successful post war ships FEARLESS and INTREPID. These craft were used to provide docking and maintenance and repair services close to the beaches. HIGHWAY was built at Newport News and was launched in July 1943. Of 4270 tons, she had a speed of 16 knots. On completion she sailed across the Atlantic and through the Mediterranean to Bombay, arriving in February 1944. She returned to the Mediterranean in April 1944 and operated off Italy and N. Africa. In December 1944 she visited Inveraray (Scotland) and then transported major landing craft to Gibraltar before returning to India. She was at Singapore in September 1945 and returned to the UK in February 1946. She was returned to the USN in April 1946.

HOOD

The battlecruiser HOOD had become famous before the war, being a handsome ship and involved in many important cruises and events. She was with the Home Fleet at the outbreak of war, coming under air attack on 26 September and later escorting convoys across the Atlantic. At the end of March 1940 she was earmarked to strengthen the Mediterranean Fleet, but she remained in Home Waters when the Norwegian campaign began. In June 1940 she became Flagship of the newly formed Force H based on Gibraltar. She covered operations to reinforce Malta and to prevent French warships falling into German hands. By November she had returned to the Home Fleet and in May 1941, when it was known that the German battleship BISMARCK was heading into the Atlantic, she, with the battleship PRINCE OF WALES and 6 destroyers headed to intercept her in the Denmark Strait. BISMARCK was sighted on the morning of 24 May, and the engagement began at 25,000 yards. The BISMARCK's first salvoes were very accurate, and a fire broke out on the HOOD, followed by a huge explosion. The HOOD sank leaving just 3 survivors. The BISMARCK was sunk three days later.

49

JEWEL

The Algerine class minesweeper JEWEL was completed in December 1944 at Belfast. The class was developed from the Halcyon class, but were beamier to allow space for more stores, fuel etc. Originally designed as wire sweepers, they later carried all types of sweep. 110 were completed and 15 cancelled, half being built in Canada. At first she operated from Granton and after work up joined her Flotilla at Scapa Flow in February 1945. She took part in a combined minesweeping and minelaying operation off Norway and in March transferred to Harwich. In June she was based on Antwerp. In September she sailed for the East Indies and in October transferred to the British Pacific Fleet operating in the North Borneo Area. She returned to the UK in September 1946 and was placed in reserve. She was with the Tay Division RNVR from 1948-1951 and joined the Dartmouth Training Squadron in 1956. She paid off in August 1961 and was broken up in 1967.

KING GEORGE V

This photograph was taken in 1948, but the battleship KING GEORGE V had had few modifications since her completion in December 1940. She was of a new class, mounting a new 14-inch gun in two quadruple and one twin mountings. For AA protection she carried twin 5.25-inch, eight barreled 2-pounders, 40-mm and 20-mm guns. She operated with the Home Fleet and in May 1941 was Flagship of the force that sank the BISMARCK. She continued to cover operations, including Russian convoys and attacks on Norway. In May 1942 she was damaged when she rammed and sank the destroyer PUNJABI. Repairs took till June. After further Russian convoys, she covered the invasions of Sicily and Salerno. After a refit to enhance her AA armament, she sailed for the East Indies, arriving in December 1944. She then took part in strikes on Sumatra before joining the British Pacific Fleet. She took part in operations off Okinawa and in July shelled targets on the Japanese mainland - the last action in which a British battleship fired her main armament at an enemy target. She was at the Japanese surrender. She returned to the UK in 1946, and after a spell in the Training Squadron was placed in reserve before being broken up in 1958.

KINGSTON

The destroyer KINGSTON was completed on 14 September 1939. On 29 November 1939 she helped sink U-35 off the Shetlands. After further anti-submarine operations, she joined the Mediterranean Fleet in May 1940, then the Red Sea Force. On 22 June she helped sink the Italian submarine EVANGELISTA TORRICELLA and five days later attacked another submarine. She escorted convoys through the Red Sea and in March 1941 took part in the capture of Berbera. In April 1941 she helped evacuate British troops from Greece and during the Battle for Crete was damaged by near misses. She took part in bombardments and covered convoys in the Mediterranean. During one convoy to Malta in March 1942, she was hit by a shell, but managed to fire 3 torpedoes at an enemy battleship and cruisers. She reached Malta for repairs, but whilst there under repair on 11 April 1942 she was bombed and broke in two.

KITTIWAKE

The patrol sloop KITTIWAKE was of the Kingfisher class, being built by Thornycroft before the war and was first commissioned on 29 April 1937. With a displacement of 530 tons, she was armed with a 4-inch gun and had a speed of 20 knots. Designed for coastal work, the class operated mainly on the East Coast protecting convoys. In August 1939 KITTIWAKE was allocated to the Reserve Fleet for the Royal Review at Portland. On 20 September 1939 she was mined in the Channel and was towed to Sheerness for repairs, which took until January 1941 to complete. She suffered collision damage in September 1941 and November 1944. For most of the war she was based on Harwich escorting East Coast convoys, but from March 1945 she operated from Antwerp. She paid off on 28 May 1945. She became the Chinese merchant ship TUCH SING in September 1946.

LAFOREY

The destroyer LAFOREY was of the LIGHTNING Class, armed with three power worked turrets of two 4.7-inch guns, and 8 torpedo tubes. Handsome ships, they had a speed of 36 knots. She completed in August 1941 and in September escorted a convoy to Malta. When the carrier ARK ROYAL was torpedoed in November 1941, LAFOREY went alongside and provided power, rescue and salvage teams. In May 1942 she took part in the Diego Suarez operation, carrying out bombardments. In August 1942, whilst escorting another convoy to Malta, she rescued survivors from the carrier EAGLE. In December 1942, after the N African landings, she escorted convoys, taking the damaged liner STRATHALLEN in tow. In spring 1943 she bombarded Tunisia and in June Pantellaria and Lampedusa. On 23 July she helped sink the Italian submarine ASCIANGHI. In September she was at the Salerno landings, being damaged by shore batteries. She continued bombardments of enemy shore installations to support the army in Italy. On 29 March 1944 she took part in a multi-ship attack on U-223 northeast of Palermo. The next morning the submarine torpedoed LAFOREY, before being sunk herself by the other ships. There were 69 survivors from LAFOREY.

LATONA
The fast minelayer LATONA was built to carry 400 mines at high speed (39.75 knots designed) to conduct lays in enemy held waters. She was completed in May 1941 at Southampton. She was armed with three twin 4-inch and one quadruple 2-pounder and multiple machine guns. She was allocated to the Mediterranean Fleet and reached Alexandria via the Cape in June 1941. On 21 July she carried out a trial run carrying personnel and cargo to Tobruk, and later took RAF personnel to Cyprus. On 25 October 1941, whilst on passage to Tobruk with personnel stores and ammunition for the relief of Australian troops at Tobruk, she came under enemy air attack. She received a direct hit in her engine room, which started a serious fire in the ammunition in the cargo. There was a heavy explosion aft and the fire became uncontrollable. LATONA had to be abandoned, and was sunk by torpedoes from the destroyer ENCOUNTER.

(World Ship Photo Library)

LCF(3)4

Landing Craft Flak were specialist vessels designed to protect other landing craft during operations during opposed beaches landings. She was a converted Landing Craft Tank of 485 tons and was powered by two Paxman diesels giving her a speed of 11 knots. Her armament comprised eight single 2-pounder guns mounted en echelon along her tank deck together with four single 20-mm mounted forward and aft. In August 1942 she took part in the Dieppe raid and was damaged. In July 1945 she paid off into reserve at Messina and was transferred to the Italian Navy in March 1946.

LCT 537

Landing Craft Tank 537 was powered by two Paxman diesel engines and could make 9.5 knots. She could carry 6 x 40-ton tanks or 9 x 30-ton tanks or 13 loaded 3 ton lorries or 350 tons of cargo. These very flexible vessels could approach beaches and land vehicles in 3 feet of water, and were also used for tending nets etc. LCT 537 was built in 1942 and was damaged in October 1943. She was paid off at Naples in January 1944 and was taken into use as a yard craft (No 3001) being used as a dumb lighter there until finally being written off in May 1953.

LST (3) 3028

Landing Ship Tank (LST) 3028 was completed in May 1945 by A Stephen & Sons, Glasgow. She was steam powered and could carry 15 x 40 ton tanks or 27 x 25 ton tanks, or 14 x 3 ton lorries and 168 troops. She displaced 2,256 tons and had a speed of 13 knots. She was armed with four twin 20-mm and two single 20-mm. The task of LSTs was to take the military across long sea passages to land them directly onto the assault beaches. This photograph was taken in 1946 in Loch Fyne. On 5 September 1946 she transferred to the War Office and was operated by the Royal Army Service Corps as the SNOWDEN SMITH. In December 1958 she was transferred to the Ministry of Transport and Civil Aviation. American counterparts of these vessels were designated LST (2) and were diesel driven. Some of these ships still survive today after nearly 60 years.

LIVERPOOL (14 October 1940)

The LIVERPOOL was in the second group of Southampton Class light cruisers. Completed in October 1938, she joined the East Indies Station, where she was at the outbreak of war, protecting trade routes. In November she operated off Japan, and in April 1940 she became Flagship of the Red Sea force. In May she transferred to the Mediterranean, and the next month was in action with Italian destroyers, of which one was sunk. She took part in the action off Calabria and on 29 July was bombed whilst escorting a convoy in the Aegean. She then escorted convoys and carried troops to Malta. While returning from an operation covering air attacks on Leros, she was torpedoed forward. A further explosion wrecked the bows, which finally broke off and sank (this photo-graph). Repairs in the USA took till January 1942. She then took part in Russian convoys. On 14 June 1942 she was escorting a convoy to Malta which came under heavy air attack well into the Mediterranean. LIVERPOOL was a prime target, and was torpedoed and badly damaged. She was taken in tow for Gibraltar, and arrived safely despite further attacks. Repairs took till July 1945. In October 1945 she rejoined the Mediterranean Fleet. She paid off in 1952 and was broken up in 1958.

LOCH CRAGGIE

The frigate LOCH CRAGGIE was one of the very successful Loch Class, whose construction was prefabricated to allow rapid building. LOCH CRAGGIE was completed in October 1944 by Harland and Wolff, being built in less than ten months. She worked up at Tobermory and then operated out of Liverpool and Londonderry, escorting convoys in the North Atlantic. On 16 January 1945 she helped sink U-482. She was allocated to the East Indies Fleet in May 1945, was refitted at Cardiff and arrived at Singapore via Ceylon on 3 October 1945. She operated out of Singapore patrolling the Dutch East Indies. She was placed in reserve at Devonport in October 1946. Refitted in 1948, she served in the Mediterranean in 1950-52 before being placed in reserve at Gibraltar. She was de-equipped in 1952, being stripped of her funnel and boiler room. She was sold for scrap in July 1963, being broken up at Lisbon.

LOCH ECK (October 1944)

The frigate LOCH ECK completed in November 1944 at Smith's Dock. She took just over a year to build. The Loch Class were based on the earlier River Class frigates, but to a simplified design to speed construction. After work up she operated out of Londonderry and took part in the sinking of U-1279 on 3 February 1945, U-989 on 14 February 1945 and U-1278 on 17 February 1945, all off the Shetlands. In May 1945 she visited Norwegian ports and was then allocated to the Eastern Fleet, arriving at Singapore on 6 October 1945 after a refit at Avonmouth. She was placed in reserve at Devonport in 1947 and in October 1948 she was transferred to the Royal New Zealand Navy and renamed HAWEA. She was sold in 1965 and was broken up at Hong Kong in 1966.

LOCH INSH

LOCH INSH was another Anti-submarine frigate of the Loch Class,, completed in October 1944 by Robb at Leith. She joined the Western Approaches Command after completion, based on Liverpool. She was on patrol on 6 December when the frigate BULLEN was sunk off Cape Wrath by U-297. She then took part in the sinking of the U-boat before sailing to escort a Russian convoy. Just before the convoy sailed from Kola on its return voyage, LOCH INSH sank U-307 in the Kola Inlet. After a refit she sailed for the East Indies in September 1945, remaining there until early 1946. She was then placed in reserve at Devonport until 1950. In 1950-52 she served in the Home Fleet and was modernised at Devonport in 1953-4, with a twin 4-inch and six 40-mm guns, and went on to serve in the East Indies and Persian Gulf. In October 1964 she was transferred to the Royal Malay Navy as the Training Ship HANG TUAH. She was sold for scrap in 1977.

LOCH QUOICH

The frigate LOCH QUOICH was completed in January 1945 at Blyth. Another of the successful Loch class frigates, she was armed with the new twin Squid ahead throwing anti-submarine mortar which proved ten times more effective than depth charges. On completion she immediately worked up at Tobermory and joined the Londonderry local escort force, escorting convoys until May 1945. She was then allocated to the Eastern Fleet and after a refit, arrived at Colombo on 4 August 1945. She reached Singapore on 24 September 1945. From 1945 to 1954 she served on the East Indies Station, being at Mombasa in November 1952 during the Mau Mau Terrorist campaign. Plans to modify her were cancelled in the early 1950s, and she was placed in reserve at Portsmouth in June 1954. She arrived at Dunston for scrap in November 1957.

MANCHESTER (June 1942)

The MANCHESTER was one of three slightly improved Southampton Class cruisers, fitted with a Flag bridge and improved main armament. She completed in August 1938 and was allocated to the East Indies, where she was serving when war was declared. She was at Malta in November 1939 and sailed for the UK. In spring 1940 she was part of the Northern Patrol and during the Norwegian campaign took part in the expedition to Namsos. She was then based on the Humber for anti-invasion duties, but in November returned to the Mediterranean to escort convoys. She refitted in UK in spring 1941, and took part in the search for the BISMARCK. After more patrols in the North, she was an escort to the Substance convoy to Malta in July 1941, during which she was hit by an aircraft torpedo. She was repaired in the USA. In June 1942 she helped cover Russian convoys and to relieve Spitzbergen. In August 1942 she again went south to escort the Pedestal convoy to Malta. At midnight 12/13 August she was torpedoed by Motor Torpedo Boats off Cape Bon. Disabled, she was scuttled and many of her crew became prisoners of war.

MATCHLESS (21 December 1944)

The destroyer MATCHLESS was in the second flotilla of the powerful Lightning Class. In March 1942 she began escorting Russian convoys and in May escorted the damaged cruiser TRINIDAD towards Iceland. The TRINIDAD was hit during air attacks and had to be sunk by MATCHLESS. In June 1942 she sailed south to escort a convoy to Malta, which came under attack by Italian cruisers and destroyers. She and MARNE damaged one destroyer, but losses were high, only 2 ships of the convoy reaching Malta. She returned to Russian convoys and also patrolled the Bay of Biscay. During one of the Russian convoys, on 26 December 1943, she was in the escort that encountered the battlecruiser SCHARNHORST. She closed to fire torpedoes but was unable to do so because of storm damage to her torpedo tubes. After a long engagement, the German was sunk and MATCHLESS rescued 6 of her crew. She continued on Russian convoy duty until June 1944. After refit she joined the Mediterranean Fleet in January 1945 and carried out bombardments of shore targets. She returned to UK in June 1946 and was placed in reserve. In 1959 she was transferred to the Turkish Navy as the KILICALI PASHA, serving until 1970.

MEYNELL (23 December 1941)

The destroyer MEYNELL was in the first group of Hunt Class escort destroyers, completed with two twin 4-inch guns. She completed in December 1940 and after work up escorted the newly completed PRINCE OF WALES to Rosyth. After escorting minelaying operations she joined the 21st Destroyer Flotilla at Sheerness, her base for the rest of the war. She had several encounters with E boats, for which she was fitted with a 2-pounder gun right forward, claiming several hits. In February 1943 she was detached to escort a convoy to Russia, encountering severe weather during which the cruiser SHEFFIELD was damaged. She then carried out a Biscay patrol before returning to the Nore. On 26 February she engaged 5 E-boats off Great Yarmouth, claiming a hit on one. She was an escort in the Eastern Task Force for the Normandy landings but in October was damaged by grounding. In March 1945 she was again in action with E-boats. In June 1945 she visited Wilhelmshaven. She then became an aircraft target ship and in 1946 visited the Mediterranean. She then was placed in reserve and was transferred to Ecuador in 1955 as the PRESIDENTE VELASCO IBARRA, being stricken in May 1978.

MILNE (16 December 1944)

The destroyer MILNE was launched by Scotts but was completed in August 1942 by Browns because of air raids. After working up she escorted Russian convoys, starting with PQ 18, which lost 12 ships to sustained air and submarine attacks. She then joined Force H for the N. African landings, providing cover against surface attacks and escorting convoys. Whilst supporting convoys in the Atlantic she rescued 143 survivors from 3 merchant ships. She returned to Russian convoy duties in February 1943 and the next month was on blockade-runner interception and convoy duty in the Bay of Biscay. Rejoining the Home Fleet she operated off Norway and took part in further Russian convoys. In April 1944 she escorted carriers on a strike against the TIRPITZ before returning once again to Russian convoy duty. On 31 May 1944 she sank U-289. She continued to cover operations off the Norwegian coast and Russian convoys until October 1944. After a refit she transferred to the Mediterranean where she took part in bombardments of the French Coast and Genoa and escorted convoys. She returned to the UK in April 1946 and was placed in reserve. In 1959 she was handed over to the Turkish Navy as the ALP ARSLAN. She went for disposal in 1970.

MOHAWK (April 1941)

This unusual photograph was taken of the destroyer MOHAWK, lying on her side in shallow water after being sunk in a sharp engagement. She, and 3 other destroyers, intercepted an enemy convoy of 5 ships escorted by 3 destroyers off Sfax Tunisia, on 16 April 1941. In a fast moving night action, two enemy destroyers and the 5 merchant ships were sunk, with the third destroyer left on fire. However, MOHAWK was torpedoed and had to be sunk. A Tribal class destroyer, she had a heavy gun armament of four twin 4.7-inch guns. When completed in September 1938. In October 1939 her bridge was damaged by bombing. She had been active in the Norwegian campaign, coming under air attack and escorting troops to Norway. She entered the Mediterranean in May 1941, escorting convoys, carrying out bombardments and supporting the Army ashore. She took part in the Battle of Cape Matapan and in April 1941 joined a striking force operating out of Malta against enemy convoys. She gained 7 Battle Honours in her short career.

MTB 208

MTB 208 was built by Whites to a Vosper's hard chine design, with a hull of double diagonal mohagany and with bonded wood decks. Of 41 tons, she was 71 feet in length, and powered by three Sterling Admiral engines giving her a speed of 36 knots. She was armed with two 21-inch torpedo tubes and had a twin 0.5-inch Vickers gun in a turret and two single 0.303-inch guns as well as two depth charges. Completed in August 1942, she took part in the Normandy landings. She is photographed here at Weymouth in 1943. The Coastal Forces base there, HMS BEE, had been commissioned in September 1942, but in October 1943 was moved to Holyhead when the south coast became overcrowded during the build up for Operation Overlord. The site was taken over by the Combined Operations Base HMS GRASSHOPPER. MTB 208 paid off in September 1944 and was earmarked for disposal in December 1944. She was sold to a private individual after the war.

NEPTUNE (July 1935)

The cruiser NEPTUNE was completed by Portsmouth Dockyard in 1934. She was on the South Atlantic Station when war was declared. She immediately carried out searches for enemy shipping, sinking the SS INN on 5 September 1939. She operated with hunting groups against raiders and enemy shipping until April 1940, when she joined the Mediterranean Fleet. In June 1940 she took part in bombardments and was in action with Italian destroyers on the 28th, when one destroyer was sunk. In July she helped cover convoys to Malta and Alexandria and was at the action off Calabria, and sank an enemy oil tanker. Despite air attacks, she was unscathed and escorted carriers taking aircraft to Malta. In August she joined the S. Atlantic Station, intercepting an enemy tanker on 8 October. She was on anti-raider patrols until February 1941, when she returned to the UK. She later returned to the Mediterranean via the Cape in June 1941. She sank a German tanker in June en route. She helped reinforce British troops in Cyprus and Tobruk. In December 1941 she was again in action with enemy forces during a convoy to Malta. On the 19th, while operating with the Malta striking force, she ran onto mines off Libya, hitting four. She capsized and sank. There was just one survivor.

NORFOLK (8 March 1945)

The NORFOLK was in the third group of the County Class heavy cruisers. She completed in 1930. In September 1939 she was with the Home Fleet and damaged by an air raid at Scapa Flow in March 1940. Repairs took till July, when she rejoined the Home Fleet and covered convoys to Iceland. In November she escorted convoys to the Cape. She patrolled the West African area looking for raiders and in March covered a Halifax convoy. In May 1941 she and SUFFOLK sighted the BISMARCK in the Denmark Strait and shadowed the German battleship, being present when the BISMARCK was sunk. In 1941 and 1942 she escorted Russian convoys. She was then off the Azores for the North African landings before returning to Russian convoys and relieving Spitzbergen. She was damaged during the action in December 1943 when the SCHARNHORST was sunk. After a refit she rejoined the Home Fleet and in January 1945 engaged an enemy convoy off Norway, sinking 2 merchant ships and 6 escorts In May 1945 she visited Bergen. In June she escorted the King of Norway to Oslo. She then sailed for the East Indies, and remained there until 1949 when she was placed in reserve, before being broken up in 1950.

NUBIAN (June 1941)

The NUBIAN was one of the large group of Tribal Class destroyers. Completed in 1938, she carried out sweeps off Norway in 1939/40. She played a full part in the Norwegian campaign, and in May 1940 joined the Mediterranean Fleet. In March 1941 she helped sink the cruiser POLA off Cape Matapan. The next month she helped destroy an enemy convoy and took part in the evacuation of Greece. In May she helped sink a convoy bound for Crete, and later had her stern blown off (see picture) while covering strikes on airfields. Nevertheless she made Alexandria at 22 knots. After repairs she joined a striking force based on Malta in November. She helped take Pantellaria and took the surrender of Linosa. She was at the landings in Sicily and Italy. In December 1943 she returned to the UK for a refit and then took part in patrols off Norway. In January 1945 she sailed for the E. Indies, covering the assault on Rangoon and the Arakan. She also took part in strikes on the Andamans, and sank a Japanese supply vessel and escort. She took part in the re-occupation of Port. Swettenham and Singapore. Returning to the UK in November 1945, she paid off and was sold in 1949. 12 of her RN sisterships had been lost in the war. She had gained 13 Battle Honours for her name during her wartime service.

OFFA

The destroyer OFFA was in the first of the Emergency War Design flotillas, based on the J Class destroyers, but with four single guns. Half the class carried 4.7-inch guns, the other half 4-inch. OFFA had 4.7-inch. She was completed by Fairfield in September 1941. In November she escorted a Russian Convoy, and was bombed - but without damage. She took part in the N. African landings and afterwards returned to Iceland. In April 1943 she was with the Third Support Group operating in the Atlantic and in July operated off N. Africa and Sicily. In November she was back at Scapa Flow, and covered further Russian convoys. On 4 May 1944, while operating off Portsmouth, she was hit by a bomb. For the Normandy landings she covered the Eastern flank of the assault forces in the Channel, and came under air attack, and took part in an action with German E-boats from Boulogne on 11/12 June. In the Autumn 1944 and April 1945 she escorted Russian convoys, and in May 1945 visited Kiel and Flensburg. She operated in European waters through 1945-46, calling at Copenhagen, Oslo and German ports. In 1949 she transferred to Pakistan and was renamed TARIQ. She was returned to the Royal Navy and broken up in 1959.

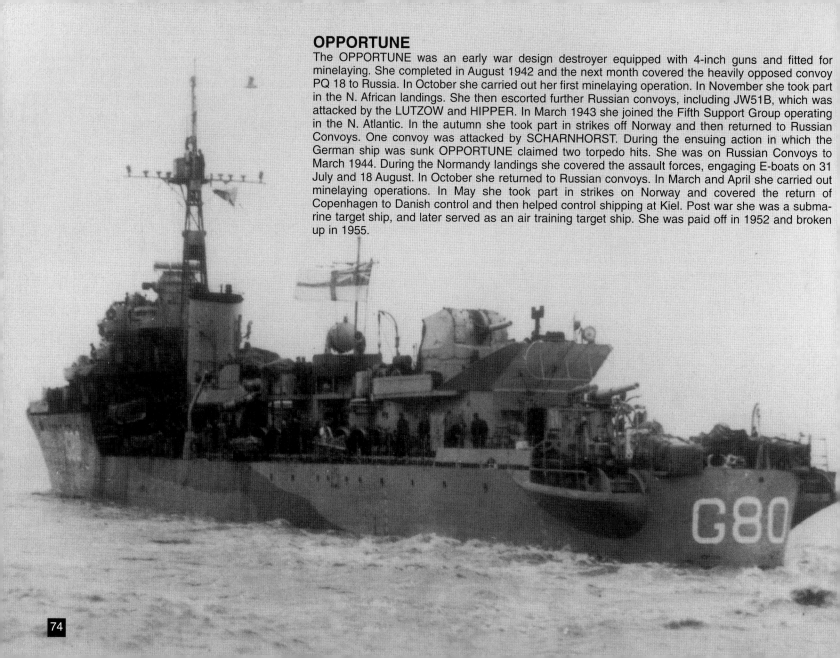

OPPORTUNE

The OPPORTUNE was an early war design destroyer equipped with 4-inch guns and fitted for minelaying. She completed in August 1942 and the next month covered the heavily opposed convoy PQ 18 to Russia. In October she carried out her first minelaying operation. In November she took part in the N. African landings. She then escorted further Russian convoys, including JW51B, which was attacked by the LUTZOW and HIPPER. In March 1943 she joined the Fifth Support Group operating in the N. Atlantic. In the autumn she took part in strikes off Norway and then returned to Russian Convoys. One convoy was attacked by SCHARNHORST. During the ensuing action in which the German ship was sunk OPPORTUNE claimed two torpedo hits. She was on Russian Convoys to March 1944. During the Normandy landings she covered the assault forces, engaging E-boats on 31 July and 18 August. In October she returned to Russian convoys. In March and April she carried out minelaying operations. In May she took part in strikes on Norway and covered the return of Copenhagen to Danish control and then helped control shipping at Kiel. Post war she was a submarine target ship, and later served as an air training target ship. She was paid off in 1952 and broken up in 1955.

OTWAY (4 April 1944)

The submarine OTWAY was built at Barrow for the Royal Australian Navy as the OA 2, completing in September 1927. Her class were the first submarines to carry ASDIC in lieu of hydrophones. Of 1,475 tons, she was armed with a 4-inch gun and eight torpedo tubes, six forward and two aft. She was transferred to the Royal Navy in 1930 and was at Malta at the outbreak of war. Initially engaged in anti-submarine exercises, she returned to the UK in February 1940 to join the Training Establishment at Portsmouth, later moving to the Clyde. She continued to take part in A/S exercises, and also trials, such as that of the Hedgehog ahead-throwing A/S weapon in November 1941. In December 1941 she was deployed lest the SCHARNHORST and GNEISENAU break out into the Atlantic, patrolling the Bay of Biscay. She was bombed on her way home in January 1942. She then returned to her training task, remaining there until May 1945. When she was paid off for scrap.

PRINCE OF WALES (5 September 1941)

The second of the King George V class battleships, the PRINCE OF WALES had just been completed at the end of March 1941. A few weeks later she sailed to stop the German battleship BISMARCK breaking out into the Atlantic. She took part in the engagement with the BISMARCK during which the HOOD was sunk. PRINCE OF WALES was damaged during the action. Three months later, in August 1941, she took Winston Churchill to meet President Roosevelt off Newfoundland. In October 1941 she sailed for Singapore via the Cape to provide a deterrent to Japanese aggression. She arrived at Singapore on 2 December. Five days later Japan attacked Pearl Harbour and invaded Siam and Malaya. On 8 December she sailed with the battlecruiser REPULSE and destroyers to prevent enemy landings. After an abortive search for assault forces, the force headed back towards Singapore, but came under heavy air attack. PRINCE OF WALES suffered an unfortunate hit early in the action, and finally was sunk by bombs and torpedoes.

QUENTIN (June 1942)

The destroyer QUENTIN was built by White and completed in April 1942. After work up she was allocated to the Eastern Fleet, escorting the battleship RODNEY to Freetown. She remained there for a period on convoy escort duty. In August 1942 she took part in the Pedestal convoy to Malta which came under heavy attack. During it she hunted a submarine. After the convoy she returned to Freetown and then escorted the battleship QUEEN ELIZABETH across the Atlantic. On 3 September 1942 she helped sink U-162 off Trinidad. She then escorted further convoys before being refitted. In October 1942 she joined Force H for the N. African landings. On 28 November 1942 she helped sink the Italian Submarine DESSIE off Bone. After the North African landings she became part of a striking force operating out of Bone. The force sank four merchantmen and a destroyer on the night 1st/2nd December 1942. They were returning to Bone when they came under air attack. During these attacks she was torpedoed and sunk, 180 of her crew were rescued by her sister ship QUIBERON.

QUORN

The destroyer QUORN was of the first group of the Hunt Class escort destroyers and completed in September 1940. She joined the Nore Command and covered convoys on the East Coast. She was attacked by aircraft and damaged by two delayed action bombs on 2 April 1941. She was then damaged by mines in the Thames Estuary on 18 August 1941. On 20 April 1942 she was again mined, which caused more damage, repairs taking 4 months. On the night of 13/14 October 1942 she took part in the attack by destroyers and motor torpedo boats on the German auxiliary cruiser Schiff 45/ KOMET in the Channel, during which the raider was sunk and two of her escorts damaged. In May 1944 she engaged 3 E-boats in the North Sea, damaging one. In June 1944 she took part in the Normandy landings and on 3 August 1944 was lost during a heavy raid on the assault forces. German aircraft dropped circling torpedoes and human torpedoes, explosive motor boats and E-boats engaged the assembled shipping. She was probably hit by a human torpedo. 130 of her crew were lost.

REVENGE (October 1940)

The battleship REVENGE had been completed in March 1916 and served at Jutland. In 1939 she was with the Home Fleet based on Portland. In October 1939 she carried bullion to Halifax, arriving safely. She then joined the Halifax Escort Force covering North Atlantic convoys against German raiders until July 1940. In August 1940 she escorted merchant ships carrying evacuees to Canada and in October 1940 carried out a bombardment of Cherbourg (this photograph- EMERALD in background). She then remained in Home Waters lest German heavy ships broke out to operate against Atlantic convoys. She was covering a convoy when the BISMARCK was sunk trying to break out into the Atlantic. In November 1941 she joined the Eastern Fleet, covering convoys in the Indian Ocean. Iin February 1943 she escorted a troop convoy from Suez to Fremantle. In September 1943 she returned to the Clyde and then became part of a training base (SHRAPNEL II) for stokers at Southampton. She moved to the Clyde (IMPERIEUSE II) in May 1944 and to Devonport (IMPERIEUSE) in December 1944. She paid off and was scrapped in 1948

RHYL

The minesweeper RHYL was a steam driven Bangor Class vessel. Of 656 tons, she carried a 3-inch gun and had a speed of 16.5 knots. She was built by Lobnitz, and completed in November 1940. Five of the class were built in Canada for the Royal Navy, and were lent to the Royal Canadian Navy. Nine of the class were transferred to the Royal Indian Navy in 1941. Note her enclosed bridge, with protective padding fitted, and her weathered paintwork. RHYL initially served on the Clyde and at Scapa Flow, but moved south to the Channel in March 1941 and later operated out of Harwich. She was one of the escorts for the Dieppe raid in August 1942. She took part in the North African landings, remaining in the Mediterranean until December 1944. She then returned to Harwich. She was broken up at Gateshead in 1948.

ST. ALBANS

The ST. ALBANS was one of fifty USN destroyers transferred to Britain in 1940. She commissioned in September 1940 and arrived in the UK in October, becoming an escort to a minelaying force. Operations took her to the Denmark Strait and she also escorted convoys. In April 1941 she was transferred to the Royal Norwegian Navy, helping to sink U-401 in August 1941. In October that year she was damaged in a gale but reached Iceland safely. In April 1942 she began escorting Russian convoys, sinking the Polish submarine JASTRZAB by accident in May. In July she was returned to the Royal Navy, and later escorted convoys in the North Atlantic. After a refit she became a target vessel for Coastal Command and afterwards became part of the Western Local Escort Force operating out of Halifax. She returned to the UK in January 1944 and was placed in reserve. In July 1944 she became the Russian DOSTOINYI, based in the Kola. She was returned from the Russians in February 1949 and broken up later that year.

81

SHEARWATER

The Kingfisher class patrol vessel SHEARWATER was in the third group of her class, being completed in September 1939 by White. These handy vessels were powered by two geared turbines, giving them a speed of 20 knots. They had a range of 5,000 miles at 10 knots. By 1940 her armament had been supplemented with 2 x 20-mm and 4 Lewis guns and by 1944 she carried a single 4-inch, two 2-pounders, two 20-mm and four Lewis guns. She was one of the Western Approaches escorts in 1939, but in 1940 operated out of Harwich on the East Coast. In October 1941 she collided with the destroyer SOUTHDOWN. In April 1942 she took the destroyer QUORN in tow when she was mined. In March 1945 she operated from Antwerp, and finally paid off in May 1945. She was broken up in 1947.

SHROPSHIRE (28 April 1942)

The cruiser SHROPSHIRE was completed in 1929. Much of her pre-war service was in the Mediterranean, where she was in 1939. In October she joined the South Atlantic Station to search for raiders and to escort convoys. In December she intercepted a German ship which scuttled itself. In February 1941 she carried out bombardments during the attack on Italian Somaliland. She returned to escort duty and in March intercepted and brought in a Vichy French ship. She joined the Home Fleet in July of that year and escorted the carrier ARGUS to Russia. In March 1942 she returned to the South Atlantic, but was recalled and, after a refit, was handed over to the Royal Australian Navy to replace the lost CANBERRA in April 1943. While with an American Task Force she bombarded South Pacific Islands and covered landings at Leyte. She attacked the Japanese battlefleet in the Suriago Strait in October 1944, obtaining several hits on a battleship. In January 1945, while at the Lingayen Gulf landings, she was attacked by suicide aircraft, shooting several down. In June 1945 she assisted with the landings at Balikpapan and was on patrol off Moratai when the war ended, and was at Sagami Bay for the formal surrender. She was laid up 1948 and was broken up in 1955.

SIDON (7 November 1944)

The SIDON was completed in November 1944. An improved S class submarine, she was armed with six torpedo tubes and had a range of 6,000 miles at 10 knots. In March 1945 she carried out a patrol, off Andoy and the next month sailed for the Far East. She arrived at Trincomalee in May. In July she sailed for her first patrol in the East, taking passage from Fremantle, where she had diverted because of battery trouble, to Subic. Off Saigon she rescued an American airman who had be adrift for 5 days. She was at the re-occupation of Hong Kong in September 1945, being relieved by TOTEM on 20 October. She then returned to the UK via Singapore and Colombo, arriving at Portsmouth in December 1945, where she paid off. In June 1955 she was alongside the MAID-STONE at Portland when a torpedo onboard exploded. SIDON sank with the loss of 13 men. She was salvaged and beached a week later. In 1957 she was sunk for use as an anti-submarine target off Portland.

SIRIUS (June 1942)

The cruiser SIRIUS was built at Portsmouth Dockyard and completed in May 1942 after delays caused by bombing. She immediately joined the Home Fleet and operated in support of Russian convoys. In August 1942 she helped escort the Pedestal convoy to Malta, which came under heavy attacks and only 5 out of 14 ships got through. She then operated in the South Atlantic on patrols and in November 1942 covered the N. African landings before joining a striking force operating out of Bone. With this force she helped sink an enemy convoys of 4 ships together with an escorting destroyer. In July 1943 she was part of the covering force for the Sicilian landings, and carried out bombardments both on Sicily and on the Italian mainland. In September she took troops to Taranto. In October she transferred to the Levant and helped destroy an enemy convoy on 7th. Later that month she was bombed and had to undergo repairs, which lasted over 4 months. She took part in the Normandy landings, then returned to the Mediterranean for the South of France landings and in September 1944 entered Toulon. She helped in the re-occupation of Athens in October 1944. She left the Mediterranean in February 1946 and was finally placed in reserve in 1949, and was broken up in 1956.

SOMALI (29 July 1939)

This picture was taken just before the war broke out, but SOMALI had only been completed in December 1938. She was one of the heavily gunned Tribal class destroyers, and she achieved 36.6 knots on trials. In 1939 she was with the Home Fleet. She took part in the Norwegian campaign and was near missed at Mo. In March 1941 she took part in the raid on the Lofoten Islands and in May 1941 took part in the operations against the BISMARCK, being one of the escorts of the battleship KING GEORGE V. She then undertook escort duties on Russian convoys. In August 1942 she went south to the Mediterranean to escort the Pedestal convoy to Malta, during which she took survivors off the crippled cruiser MANCHESTER. She returned to Russian convoys in September 1942, and on the 20th was torpedoed by U-703 and disabled. She was taken in tow by her sister, ASHANTI, but sank four days later when the weather worsened.

SPEARHEAD

The SPEARHEAD was an improved S Class submarine. Of 715 tons, she was armed with 6 bow torpedo tubes and a 3-inch gun. She had a surfaced speed of 14.75 knots and a submerged speed of 9 knots, and a range of 6,000 miles at 10 knots. She completed in December 1944 and operated from the Clyde. From 21 March to 1 April 1945 she patrolled off Kors Fjord, sighting a U-boat but was unable to close to attack. She was allocated to the Eastern Fleet, and called at Malta in May 1945, passed through Suez and arrived at Trincomalee in June. In July she undertook her first Eastern patrol, which was a special operation, towing the midget submarine X-4 to cut the telegraph cables from Saigon to Hong Kong and from Saigon to Singapore. The operation was a complete success, SPEARHEAD recovering X-4 and towed her back to Brunei Bay. She undertook air sea rescue duties off Singapore. She was at Hong Kong in October, and Singapore in November, returning to Portsmouth on 5 December 1945. She paid off late in December. In 1948 she was sold to Portugal and named NEPTUNO, being broken up in 1967.

STARLING

The sloop STARLING is best known as Captain Walker's ship in the Battle of the Atlantic. She was of the modified Black Swan Class of sloops and was armed with three twin 4-inch guns. She completed in April 1943 and joined the Second Escort Group, and while with that group took part in the sinking of 14 U-boats, three, U-202, U-119 and U-961 being sunk by STARLING single handedly. During the Normandy landings the Group operated in the Western Approaches to keep the assault areas clear of submarines. Three of her kills took place in this area between 31 July and 11 August. In October 1944 she left the Group, for a refit ready for the Far East. However, because of renewed U-boat activity she joined the 22nd Escort Group based on Liverpool. In January 1945 she helped sink U-482, giving her a total of 15 kills. At the end of the war she was placed in reserve and then was disarmed became a tender to the Navigation School from 1946 until 1959. She was broken up in 1965.

SUFFOLK (27 July 1940)

The heavy cruiser SUFFOLK was completed in 1928. She joined the Home Fleet in late September 1939 having been fitted with one of the first operational radar sets. She escorted convoys and was in the Northern Patrol. In April she took a force to the Faeroes and later that month intercepted a German tanker. She bombarded Stavanger airport and then came under heavy air attacks, returning with her stern under water. Repairs took until March 1941, when she rejoined the Home Fleet. In May she located and shadowed the BISMARCK. In August she escorted the first Russian convoy and in October brought bullion from Archangel to the UK. She remained with the Home Fleet till December 1942, when she was refitted for the Eastern Fleet. In summer 1943 she patrolled in the Cape area and then in the Indian Ocean. In May 1944 she took part in the air strike on Sourabaya and in October bombarded the Nicobar Islands. In January 1945 she escorted air strikes on Sumatra and from April to June covered the assault on Rangoon and bombarded Cap Nicobar and Port. Blair. In July 1945 she returned to the UK and was used on trooping tasks to June 1946. She was then placed in reserve and broken up in 1948.

SUNFISH

The submarine SUNFISH was in the first group of the S Class completing at Chatham Dockyard in July 1937. She was the prototype for the Improved S Class, and was fitted with prototype Admiralty diesel engines, giving her an improved surfaced speed of 15 knots. She was armed with six bow torpedo tubes and a 3-inch gun. On 9 and 10 April 1940 she sank steamers off the Skagerrak. In January 1941 she landed an agent during a patrol on the Norwegian Coast. In September she was refitting on the Tyne when she was damaged in an air raid and had to be towed to Portsmouth for further repairs - which took to August 1943. In May 1944 she was transferred to Russia and "renamed" B-1. On 27 July 1944 she was sunk by a Liberator of No. 86 Squadron RAF whilst on passage from Dundee to Murmansk.

TACITURN

The TACITURN was a welded submarine, completed at Barrow in October 1944. She served at Rothesay and Lerwick and carried out her first patrol whilst working up in northern waters. In February she visited Gibraltar and in April arrived at Colombo. In May 1945 she carried out a patrol in the Java Sea and South China Sea during which she fired 205 rounds from her 4-inch gun at targets, including a Japanese submarine chaser. She covered 8,753 miles on the 45-day patrol. In July she operated in the western Java Sea with her sister THOROUGH, sinking two schooners and firing on shore batteries. She reached Fremantle in August. In October she was at Hong Kong and in December at Singapore. In February 1946 she returned to Holy Loch. She was modernised and streamlined at Chatham starting in 1948, her length being increased by 14 feet to become the first "Super T". She was broken up in 1971.

TEES (September 1943)

The River Class frigate TEES was built at Aberdeen, completing in August 1943. 16 months after being laid down. 167 of these ships had been ordered, including 78 for the Royal Canadian Navy and 22 for the Royal Australian Navy. They were designed for North Atlantic escort work, being armed with two single 4-inch guns, four 20-mm guns a, Hedgehog mortars and depth charges, and with a speed of 20 knots. After work up at Tobermory, she escorted convoys to West Africa, and operated from Lagos and Freetown until July 1944. After a refit on the Tyne in August 1944 she worked up again and operated from Falmouth and Plymouth in early 1945 before returning to West Africa. She returned to the UK in June 1945 and paid off. She was laid up at Dartmouth, Harwich and then Barrow before being broken up at Newport in 1955.

THISTLE

The THISTLE was a Triton Class submarine completed in July 1939 at Barrow. She was armed with 10 torpedo tubes (8 bow and 2 amidships- all firing forward) carried 16 torpedoes and was fitted with a 4-inch gun. She had a surface speed using diesel engines of 15.25 knots, and submerged on electric motors of 8.75 knots. She joined the 2nd Flotilla at Rosyth and operated against the German Fleet in the Norwegian campaign. She attacked U-4 unsuccessfully whilst on her way to attack shipping in Stavanger harbour. Being short of torpedoes, THISTLE reverted to a patrol off Skudesnes. The next day, 10 April, THISTLE was on the surface and sighted by U-4 , who torpedoed and sank her. There were no survivors.

TRIBUNE

The submarine TRIBUNE was in the third group of the T Class. She was completed in October 1939. In January 1940 fired a full salvo of torpedoes at a U-boat off the Skaw - but missed. In August she was on anti-submarine patrol north west of Scotland and carried out another attack on a submarine, and heard explosions, but her claim was later discounted. In December she operated in the Bay of Biscay. In February 1941 she was used as an escort in the N. Atlantic, being at Halifax in April. In July 1942 she provided distant cover for Convoy PQ-17 to Russia operating from Polyarno. In October she sailed from Gibraltar to patrol off Toulon for the N.African landings, later operating from Algiers. In January 1943 she patrolled off Corsica and Toulon, and in February and March off Naples. She returned to the UK in April 1943 and operated from the Clyde from August that year. She had paid off by November 1945 and was broken up in 1947.

TRINIDAD

The TRINIDAD was completed in October 1941, one of the first group of Colony Class cruisers, armed with four triple 6-inch guns. She was built at Devonport Dockyard. In January 1942 she was an escort to a Russian convoy which was attacked by U-boats. In March she was on another Russian convoy, of which 14 of the 19 ships in convoy reached harbour despite heavy air, submarine and surface vessel attacks. On 29 March TRINIDAD and the destroyer ECLIPSE encountered 3 enemy destroyers and sank one and damaged the others. TRINIDAD was hit by one of her own torpedoes but she reached the Kola Inlet under her own power. After temporary repairs, she sailed for the UK on 13 May. The next day she was attacked by aircraft, and one hit set off a serious fire, and a near miss destroyed the temporary repairs to her previous damage. On fire and flooding, she had to be abandoned and was sunk by the destroyer MATCHLESS.

TRITON (20 June 1939)

The first member of her class, TRITON was completed at Barrow in November 1938. She was of a new patrol type, with a 42-day endurance. She was two feet longer than later vessels of the class, with a bluff bow, high bridge and eight bow torpedo tubes. She was at Portsmouth in early September 1939 and then transferred to Dundee for patrols. On 10 September she encountered the submarine OXLEY off Norway and sank her by mistake. On 10 April 1940 she encountered a fifteen-ship convoy off Norway, sinking three of them. In September 1940 she was sent to Gibraltar to reinforce the Mediterranean Fleet, and in October was at Malta. On 18 December she was lost in the Adriatic, possibly as a result of hitting a mine.

TURPIN (29 November 1944)

The TURPIN was completed in December 1944 at Chatham Dockyard. She was of welded construction, and had 11 torpedo tubes, three of which were external and faced aft. In December 1944 she had a collision with the SIDON whilst submerged. From 30 March to 10 April 1945 she carried out a patrol off Kors Fjord. She then sailed for the Far East, calling at Malta in June and arriving at Fremantle in October. In October she was at Hong Kong and in January 1946 at the Fleet Base at Manus. She visited Sydney in February 1946. In the early 1950s she was modernised and streamlined. In 1958 she had an engine failure and had to be towed 5,200 miles from Jamaica to the UK. In 1964 she was the last submarine based on Malta, and that December was sold to become the Israeli LEVIATHAN. She was broken up in 1975.

ULSTER

The Emergency war Design destroyer ULSTER joined the Home Fleet after completion in June 1943. This class of destroyers was the first completed with lattice masts. She took part in operations off Norway before taking part in Biscay patrols. In October 1943 she was in action with German destroyers in the Channel, obtaining hits on the enemy. She was damaged and repaired at Devonport. In November she joined the Mediterranean Fleet, operating off Algiers and later off the Yugoslavian Coast. She took part in coastal bombardments and was at the Anzio landings in January 1944. In May 1944 she rejoined the Home Fleet for the Normandy landings, escorting an assault convoy and carrying out bombardments off Gold Beach, before being damaged when she grounded. Later she took part in anti-submarine operations in northern waters. In December 1944 she sailed for Australia and joined the British Pacific Fleet. On 1 April, whilst operating in support of the Okinawa landings, she was damaged by a near miss. She was taken in tow for Leyte by the cruiser GAMBIA. She returned to the UK via the Panama Canal, starting a refit in August 1945. In the mid-1950s she was converted to a fast anti-submarine frigate and was eventually broken up in 1980.

UPSHOT

The U Class were the smallest submarines built in the 1930s. Their success led to further developments during the war, and UPSHOT was a modified U Class vessel and part of the fourth type of the class. She was slightly longer than earlier boats, and was of partly welded construction allowing her to dive deeper. She was armed with four torpedo tubes and a 3-inch gun. She had a surface speed of 13 knots and a dived speed of 9 knots. She completed in May 1944 at Barrow, just over one year after being laid down. She then operated out of Tobermory, Holy Loch, Rothesay and Holyhead with the Seventh Flotilla on anti-submarine training until November 1945. She was laid up at Lisahally in February 1946 and de-equipped in October 1948. She was then allocated for ship target trials prior to being broken up in 1949.

VENERABLE

A Light Fleet Carrier, VENERABLE completed in January 1945. After work up and trials she sailed for the Mediterranean and then on to the Far East, arriving in Ceylon in June 1945. She reached Sydney in July, where her 20-mm guns were exchanged for 40-mm to cope with expected Kamikaze attacks during the planned invasion of the Japanese mainland. On VJ Day she sailed from Sydney with a Task group to re-occupy Hong Kong. She provided fighter cover for the force, keeping a continuous air cover over the force until 2 September. She left Hong Kong in October 1945, repatriating ex-Prisoners of War to India. For the next few months she was kept busy moving troops and ex-prisoners, returning to Sydney at the end of December 1945, having steamed 25,000 miles since leaving. She returned to Devonport in March 1946 and in May became the Dutch KAREL DOORMAN. In 1968 she was sold to Argentina, being renamed VEINTICINCO DE MAYO. She was sold in 1998 and broken up in 1999.

VERULAM (22 January 1945)

The destroyer VERULAM was completed in December 1943. She was armed with four 4.7-inch guns, eight torpedo tubes and depth charges. She immediately went to Scapa Flow, returning south for the Normandy landings, where she escorted an assault convoy to Sword beach and escorted the battleship RAMILLIES. Afterwards she returned to Scapa and in spring 1945 was allocated to the Eastern Fleet. She called at Gibraltar in March and reached Tricomalee in April. On night 15/16 May she was with the Flotilla that sank the Japanese cruiser HAGURO in the Malacca Strait - VERULAM closing to within a mile of the enemy before firing her torpedoes, and achieving at least one hit. In August 1945 she escorted minesweepers into Penang for the Japanese surrender and on 11 September arrived at Singapore. She returned to the UK in December. In the early 1950s she was converted to a fast anti-submarine frigate and later became a trials ship, paying off in 1970 after 27 years service. She was broken up in 1972.

VICTORIOUS (24/28 July 1941)

The VICTORIOUS was the third of the Illustrious class of Fleet Carriers, completing in April 1941. Almost at once she sailed in the search for the BISMAR-CK, her aircraft obtaining a torpedo hit on the German battleship. In June she ferried aircraft to Malta. She then operated off Norway and covered convoys to Russia. In August 1942 she came south again to take part in the Pedestal convoy to Malta. During heavy air attacks she was hit by a bomb, which did not explode. She took part in the North African landings, her aircraft sinking U-517. She then refitted in the USA and was lent to the US Navy for Pacific oper-ations. In 1944 she was with the Home Fleet helping the strikes on the TIRPITZ, and later sailed East. In July and September 1944 she took part in strikes on Sumatra, and in October on the Nicobar Islands. In February 1945 she again struck at Sumatra before transferring to the Pacific. In March she attacked the Ryukyu Islands and in May she was hit by 2 Kamikaze aircraft while attacking Sakishima-Gunto. but resumed flying operations in an hour. She returned to the UK in October 1945. After the war she was in the Training Squadron, and underwent a major reconstruction between 1951-58. She was broken up in 1969.

VINEYARD

The VINEYARD was completed in August 1944 at Barrow. Of 545 tons and armed with four torpedo tubes and a 3-inch gun, she was a later version of the small U Class of submarines. This version of the U Class was able to dive a further 100 ft, to 300 ft, than earlier versions. She had a finer bow and stern and was slightly longer. She transferred to the Free French Forces in June 1944 and was renamed DORIS, after a French submarine torpedoed by U-4 on 9 May 1940 whilst operating out of Harwich with the Tenth Flotilla. After working up on the Clyde and at Rothesay, she arrived at Algiers in December 1944. She visited Malta and Oran and arrived at Toulon on 27 February 1945. She remained in the Mediterranean throughout the rest of the war. She was returned to the Royal Navy in 1947 and broken up in 1950.

WALLACE (1939)

The destroyer WALLACE was completed in 1919 as a destroyer leader. She was armed with five 4.7-inch guns, which her class introduced to destroyers. She also carried 6 torpedo tubes and achieved 37.8 knots on trials. Between the wars she served in the Baltic, Atlantic and Mediterranean. In June 1938 she started a conversion to become an escort vessel, which completed in June 1939. She was then armed with two twin high angle 4-inch, and two multiple machine guns, together with depth charge throwers and rails. Later she was also given six 2-pounders and four 20-mm guns. She was allocated to the Liverpool RNVR and, when war was declared, was put on convoy duty between Rosyth and Sheerness, which she continued until March 1945, with one small break in 1943. Throughout, she helped rescue survivors and fought off U-boats, aircraft and E-boats. In May 1943 she was fitted with radar and then escorted a convoy to Gibraltar. Afterwards she took part in the invasion of Sicily, providing fire support to troops ashore. She returned to her East Coast convoy duties in August 1943. In March 1945 she was in collision with FARNDALE and was paid off that month, placed in reserve and sent for scrap in May 1945.

WELLINGTON

The sloop WELLINGTON completed in January 1935 and served on the New Zealand Station, where she was based when war broke out. Armed with two single 4.7-inch guns, a 3-inch AA gun and machine guns, she had geared turbines giving her a speed of 16.5 knots. She returned to the UK via Singapore, and, after a refit at Cardiff when depth charge rails were fitted, she escorted convoys off Freetown and then the Western Approaches. Later she was equipped with a Hedgehog A/S mortar and radar. She took a fast convoy to North Africa in November 1942, operating there until July 1943 before returning to West Africa. After a refit in Bermuda and the Clyde when her 3-inch gun in B position was removed and she was given six Oelikons before she returned to West Africa. She accepted the surrender of U-541 in May 1945. She paid off in August 1945 before, in February 1947, she was purchased by the Honorable Co. of Master Mariners and became a floating Livery Hall on the Thames, where she remains today (2002).

WESTMINSTER (1940)

The destroyer WESTMINSTER was completed in May 1918 with four single 4-inch guns and six torpedo tubes. She served with the battlecruiser force at Rosyth before becoming part of the escort for the German high Seas Fleet when it was brought to Rosyth in November 1918. Between the wars she served in the Baltic and Atlantic. She was converted to a "Wair" escort vessel between June 1939 and January 1940, emerging with two twin high angle 4-inch guns and a new bridge. She then escorted East Coast convoys. In May she operated off Dunkirk and Belgium, and came under air attack. Damaged when she struck a wreck. She was dry docked in Dunkirk before being towed to Dover. Repairs completed in July and she then operated with the Rosyth Escort Force in the North Sea. Apart from air attacks, she was also engaged in 4 actions with E-boats, claiming to have sunk a total of three of them. After VE Day she was employed on courier duties to Norway until being reduced to Reserve at Rosyth in June 1945. She was broken up in 1948.

WHIMBREL

The sloop WHIMBREL was of the Black Swan Class, armed with three twin 4-inch guns and with a speed of 19.25 knots. She was built by Yarrows and completed work up in February 1943. She then joined the famous Second Escort Group. In June 1943 she transferred to the Seventh Escort Group and covered convoys to Gibraltar and Canada. After a refit she rejoined the Second Escort Group and carried out a Russian convoy. She then helped cover the entrance to the English Channel for the Normandy landings. Afterwards she operated in the Atlantic and was allocated to the British Pacific Fleet, arriving at Colombo in March 1945 and Manus in May. She was part of the escort for the Fleet Train, comprising tankers, ammunition ships and transport/escort carriers, for the Sakashima-Gunto Group operations, and was at the surrender in Tokyo Bay. She remained in the Pacific until the end of 1946. She was then paid off and in November 1949 was transferred to Egypt as the EL MALEK FAROUQ, and later renamed TARIK. She was deleted in 1999 and was for sale in 2002.

WHIRLWIND

WHIRLWIND was an emergency war design destroyer completed in July 1944. The class could be distinguished by their single light director aft of the bridge. After working up at Scapa Flow she sailed for the east, arriving at Malta in October and Trincomalee in December. She was in Australia in February 1945 and sailed for Manus from Sydney to join Task Force 57, operating off Leyte and Okinawa, covering air attacks and bombardments. On 30 August she was with the force that re-occupied Hong Kong. She returned to the UK in June 1946. In the early 1950s she was converted to a fast anti-submarine frigate and in 1970 became a target, eventually being sunk in 1974.

WIZARD

The destroyer WIZARD was completed in March 1944. She then joined the Home Fleet at Scapa Flow and operated off the Norwegian coast. On 9 June 1944, whilst providing cover for the Normandy landings, she was damaged in an accident by her own depth charges - repairs taking to May 1945. She then sailed to join the British Pacific Fleet, arriving at Trincomalee in July 1945, and leaving Sydney on 22 August. She is seen here refueling from the US battleship NORTH CAROLINA (though it is possible the pendant lists are incorrect and this is WRANGLER). She was at Tokyo Bay for the Japanese surrender and returned to the UK, passing through the Suez Canal in January 1946. In the early 1950s she was converted to a fast anti-submarine frigate and later joined the Dartmouth Training Squadron. She paid off in late 1965 and was broken up in 1967.

WRANGLER

The WRANGLER was built as a destroyer, completing at Barrow in July 1944. This was the last group of the emergency war design destroyers completed with 4.7-inch guns. She served in the Home Fleet and then sailed for the British Pacific Fleet, calling at Gibraltar in October 1944, Trincomalee in December and then to Manus. She joined Task Force 37 in July 1945 and was at Tokyo Bay for the Japanese surrender. In 1951-52 she was converted to a fast anti-submarine frigate, and sailed for the Mediterranean. In August 1953 she was the first ship to arrive with relief stores for the earthquake victims in the Ionian Islands. She paid off in 1955 and was refitted. In 1956 she transferred to the South African Navy and renamed VRYSTAAT. She was sunk as a target off South Africa in 1976.

ZEST (12 December 1944)

The destroyer ZEST was completed in July 1944 by Thornycroft. This class were armed with four 4.5-inch guns, eight 20-mm guns and 8 torpedo tubes and they introduced a new, single, heavy, gunnery director on their bridge. However, her main armament and director were not available when she completed, so she operated without until October 1944. After working up she joined the 27th Destroyer Flotilla of the Home Fleet and covered Russian convoys, rescuing 203 survivors from the torpedoed carrier NABOB. After operations in the Western Approaches, she rejoined the Home Fleet and returned to Russian convoy duty. In February she helped rescue the Norwegians at Soroy. In April she and other destroyers intercepted and severely mauled an enemy escorted convoy. In May 1945 she accompanied the cruisers DIDO and BIRMINGHAM and her sister ships ZODIAC and ZEALOUS to Copenhagen for the surrender of German naval units there. In late 1945 she was refitted and then worked up in the Mediterranean before returning to the Home Fleet and became a training ship. In 1953-55 she was converted to a fast anti-submarine frigate. She finally paid off in 1968 and was broken up in 1970.

INDEX